W9-AKD-941

DATE DUE

OC 24 '88			
FE 21 '91			
AP 02 '96			

LET'S VISIT IRAN

Let's visit
IRAN

GARRY LYLE

BURKE

ACKNOWLEDGEMENTS

The Publishers and Author are grateful to the following individuals and organisations for permission to reproduce copyright photographs in this book:
The Reverend J. C. Allen; M. Beamant; M. Howarth; the Iranian Information and Toursm Centre; Iranian Oil Services Ltd.; D. Martin and Christine Osborne.

CIP data
Lyle, Garry
   Let's visit Iran – 2nd ed.
   1. Iran – Social life and customs – Juvenile literature
   I. Title
   955'.05   DS266

ISBN 0 222 01038 X

Burke Publishing Company Limited
Pegasus House, 116-120 Golden Lane, London EC1Y 0TL, England.
Burke Publishing (Canada) Limited
Registered Office: 20 Queen Street West, Suite 3000, Box 30, Toronto, Canada M5H 1V5.
Burke Publishing Company Inc.
Registered Office: 333 State Street, PO Box 1740, Bridgeport, Connecticut 06601, U.S.A.
Filmset in Baskerville by Graphiti (Hull) Ltd., Hull, England.
Printed in Singapore by Tien Wah Press (Pte.) Ltd.

Contents

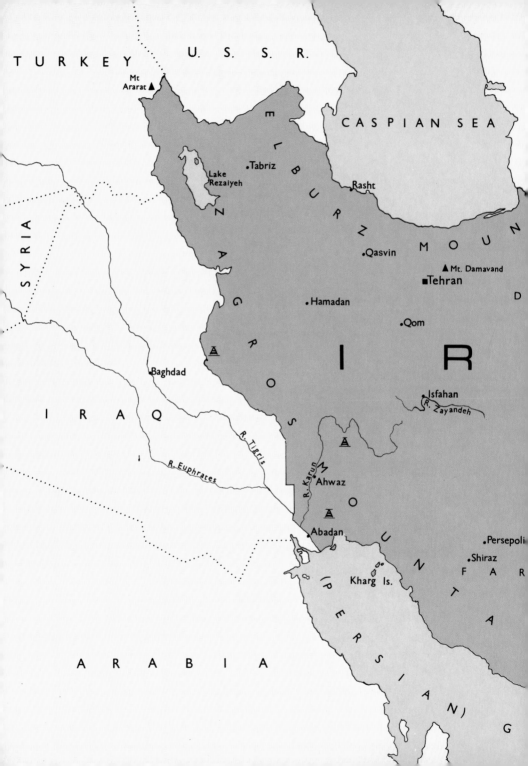

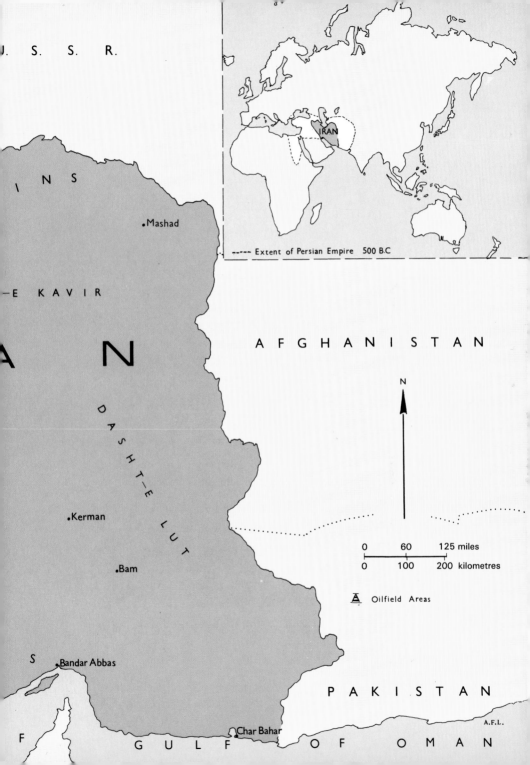

U. S. S. R.

INS

•Mashad

—E KAVIR

A

N

AFGHANISTAN

Extent of Persian Empire 500 B.C

IRAN

D A S H T — E   L U T

•Kerman

•Bam

N

0   60   125 miles
0   100   200 kilometres

Oilfield Areas

S

•Bandar Abbas

PAKISTAN

A.F.L.

F

Char Bahar

G U L F   O F   O M A N

The volcano Mount Damavand — the highest mountain in Iran

Iran on the Map

If this book had been written before the Second World War, it would almost certainly have had a different title—the title *Let's Visit Persia*. Even now, Persia is a more familiar name than Iran to many people, and it has not gone completely out of use. The Iranians themselves call their main language Farsi, which is their own modern way of saying Parsi, or Persian. Oil from the rich wells of south-western Iran is exported down a long, hot sea-road once called the Persian Gulf. The colourful woollen carpets for which Iran is famous are still called Persian carpets. And, although most cat experts say that both names are wrong, we still call a long-haired cat a Persian, not an Iranian.

However, Iran is not a new name. It is even older than the name Persia. In fact, it has been used for a longer period than the present name of any other country. Nobody knows just when it was given to the vast spread of rocky mountains, dry uplands and salty deserts between the Persian Gulf and the Caspian Sea. But we do know that it came from some tribes of horse-breeding herdsmen who settled on the uplands more than three thousand years ago. One of these tribes, the Parsa, made their home in the south-west, high above the Persian Gulf. Here, they grew so powerful and warlike that their leaders became kings of all Iran, and then conquered other countries far to the east and west. In the west, they even crossed from Asia into Europe and Africa. This began one of the greatest of the world's early empires. Because the rulers of the empire came from the Parsa people, the rest of the world gave Iran some names which meant Parsa-land. One such name was Persia; most western countries continued to use that name right up to 1935. Then, the Iranian government said that they wanted their country to have only one name. So foreigners at last began to call Iran what the Iranians themselves had always called it.

The real Parsa-land was a fairly small part of Iran that is now the province of Fars. It is centred on the upland city of Shiraz, about 180 kilometres (110 miles) from the Persian Gulf, and about 1,525 metres (5,000 feet) above sea-level. Near Shiraz, the uplands rise to wild and rocky mountains. These are part of the wide Zagros Ranges, which wall the whole of upland Iran on its western and southern sides—a distance of some 2,250 kilometres (1,400 miles).

The Zagros reach heights of over 4,500 metres (14,750 feet), and at their northern end join the Elburz Range, which rises even higher. Its tallest peak, the volcano Mount Damavand, stands 5,775 metres (18,934 feet), above sea-level. Compared to some peaks of other Asian countries—Mount Everest in Nepal, for instance—Mount Damavand may not seem particularly high. But it is about one kilometre (0.6 mile) higher than the highest mountains in Europe, and less than 305 metres (1,000 feet) below the highest in Africa and North America. Almost in the centre of the Elburz, Mount Damavand's snowy, pointed summit looks across lower peaks to Tehran, Iran's capital city.

In a salt desert

Curving round the southern end of the Caspian Sea, the Elburz Range adds a third mountain wall to upland Iran, but the fourth side—the east—is more open. There are mountains here, too, but they are much lower than the Elburz and the Zagros, and slope away to vast deserts of sand, stones and salt. Iran has a total area of about 1,648,000 square

Uplands in the dry season

A tanker going over the Zagros Mountains on the road from the oilfields to the uplands

kilometres (636,000 square miles), and the deserts of the eastern uplands fill about one-sixth of this area.

At first glance, much of the western uplands could be mistaken for more desert—especially during the long summer. Then there is no rain, and no water in most of the mountain streams, and a dry wind blows so often that Iranians call it the "Hundred and Twenty Day Wind". However, up to 30 centimetres (12 inches) of rain fall during the other seasons, and this is quite enough to raise good grass for animals. It is also enough for farmers in most areas to grow wheat, barley and some other grains; but those who live near the mountains can grow a wider variety of crops, because they have a more regular supply of water. It comes from the enormous

12

quantities of snow which fall on the upper ridges of the mountains. When the snow thaws, much of the water flows downhill to the lower slopes, and seeps underground. There, farmers tap it by digging wells. Then they lead it to their fields and villages through tunnels, sometimes as much as 80 kilometres (50 miles) long. They dig tunnels rather than irrigation canals because water in open canals would evaporate in the hot dry months, like so many of the mountain streams.

These water tunnels (called *qanats*,) have been used by Iranian farmers since very early times, and they were also dug to give towns a permanent water supply. That is why most of the upland towns—including the capital Tehran—lie on or near the lower slopes of the mountains. The few towns further away are on natural oases—green "islands" to which water comes underground without the help of qanats.

Iran looks very different on the northern side of the Elburz, where the mountains slope down to the Caspian Sea. The Caspian Sea is in fact a lake—the largest in the world—and its southern shores make about 640 kilometres (400 miles) of the border between Iran and the U.S.S.R. Between the shores and the foothills runs a low-lying plain, up to 112 kilometres (70 miles) wide, and very well-watered. Clouds which cannot get over the high mountains above give it as much as 200 centimetres (79 inches) of rain a year, spread over all seasons. Unlike the uplands, which have very hot summers but very cold winters, this Caspian plain is warm throughout the year, and so is an area of tall forests, and farms which grow such crops

13

as rice and tea. Those crops make the area particularly useful to the Iranians, because they eat a great deal of rice, and their favourite drink is tea.

On the outer side, the Zagros Ranges also slope down to a low-lying plain; this one extends along the coast of the Gulf. Here too the weather is never very cold. Indeed, it is extremely hot and humid for much of the year; but the rainfall is low, and so most of the land is barren. It is also unhealthy and—like the rest of Iran—within an earthquake belt. The latest earthquake here was in March 1977, near the old port of Bandar Abbas, Britain's first trading-station in Iran. Towards the foothills of the Zagros, the plain becomes more fertile, and farmers in some of the valleys grow sugar-cane, cotton and dates. The hottest part of this coastal plain is at the head of the

Oasis village in a desert area

Gulf, where the shade temperature in summer reaches 51 degrees Centigrade (124 degrees Fahrenheit). The plain, which is called Khuzestan, spreads northward along the border between Iran and its western neighbour Iraq, and is crossed by the Karun, Iran's only navigable river. In the days of the ancient Persian Empire, the waters of the Karun were used to irrigate the land and keep it fertile, but in later centuries Khuzestan was taken over by people who were not much interested in growing crops. They destroyed some of the irrigation canals, and allowed the rest to silt up. So the land became a dry desert for most of the year, and a desert of mud in the spring when the Karun sank it in floodwaters. However, Iran's main oil-fields are in Khuzestan. Since they were discovered, the government has dammed the rivers to control floods and make the land fertile again.

Although they are citizens of Iran, most of the people in Khuzestan are not true Iranians, but Arabs. They are decended from Arabs who moved into Iran more than a thousand years ago, but they have not mixed with the Iranians very much, and they still speak Arabic. Many of the people who live further down the Gulf, and on offshore islands, are also of Arab stock.

All told, the Arabs of Iran number more than 2,000,000, and among the country's total population of about 41,000,000 there are several million other citizens who are not true Iranians. They still speak the languages that their ancestors

Folk dancers in traditional nomad costume at a festival in Shiraz

brought to Iran many centuries ago. They are mainly Armenians, Kurds, Jews, Turks and some others whose ancestors may have come into the country with the first Iranians, if not before them.

The Armenians and Jews lead ordinary family lives, in towns and on farms, but many of the others still live as tribes of herdsmen, often in tents or temporary huts rather than houses. Some of them also live the kind of life that has been called "vertical nomadism"—that is, they graze their animals high in the mountains during the summer, and drive them down to warm lowlands near the coast before the snow comes again.

Their animals are mainly sheep and goats which they keep for meat, milk, wool and the goat-hair material used for making their tents. Sheep and goats are kept by many settled farmers, too. In fact, Iran has about twice as many of these animals as it has people. It also has a very large number of horses, donkeys and mules. These are used as working animals, because there is much less motor transport and motorised farm machinery in Iran than there is in western countries, in spite of the oil-wells.

Where there is enough water to keep them happy, water-buffaloes are used as working animals, too. In the drier parts of the country, there are many thousands of working camels. Some people believe that the Iranians were the first people to ride camels and use them as beasts of burden. It is certain that the two-humped camel came from Bactria, a part of old Iran that is now in neighbouring Afghanistan. But camels need not be used for work alone, as you can see from this old recipe:

Take about six chickens, one whole sheep or goat, and one whole camel, all carefully cleaned and dressed for cooking. Also take fifty eggs, twenty pounds of rice, ten pounds of mixed shelled nuts, and four ounces of hot spices. Boil the chickens until they are tender, and then boil the rice and the eggs. Fry the nuts and mix them with the boiled rice, adding the spices. Now stuff each chicken with some of the rice mixture, and an egg, hard-boiled and shelled. Then stuff the sheep or goat with the chickens, packing them round with more rice and eggs. When it will hold no more, stuff the camel with it, filling the spaces with the rest of the rice and eggs. Then roast your stuffed camel well, over a large open fire.

Apart from the spices, all the ingredients for that dish of stuffed camel are produced by the farmers and herdsmen of

**Nomad women
and children**

Iran. They could also provide some beef for the stuffing if there were room for it, as they graze about seven million cattle for meat, milk and leather. However, very few of them could—or would—offer any kind of pig-meat. Ninety-nine out of every hundred Iranians follow the Muslim religion, and it is a rule of their religion that they must not eat, or even handle, food that comes from a pig.

That helps to explain why there are still plenty of boar among Iran's wild animals. Another reason is that much of the country is still uncultivated and uninhabited. Some parts are so rugged and so hard to reach that they probably never will be cultivated or peopled, and this leaves room for wild animals that have died out in some of their other homelands. If you could reach the forbidding places where they live, you would find bears, lynxes, leopards, jackals, wolves and possibly even an odd lion or tiger. There are also wild creatures which are much easier to find—gazelles, for instance, and singing birds called bulbuls; and, in the Caspian Sea, colonies of seals.

Because the fiercer wild animals live in such remote places, they do very little harm. The really harmful animals are ordinary sheep and goats—especially goats. This is not because Iranian sheep and goats are any more dangerous to people

A work camel —it is thought that the Iranians were the first people to use camels as beasts of burden

than other sheep and goats, but because their eating habits destroy vegetation that Iran cannot afford to lose. Much of the mountain soil is very shallow. Plants help to hold it together. When the plants are destroyed it breaks up and is carried away by wind or rain or melting snow, leaving bare rock behind it. So, in spite of its long dry seasons, Iran would be more fertile and more thickly wooded now if it had not been feeding so many hungry sheep and goats for such a long time.

However, the animals were not entirely to blame. People in need of fuel have also done much to make parts of Iran so bare and barren. Today, many Iranians cook, and keep themselves warm in winter, with fuels from their oil-wells, and with natural gas that is found near the oil-wells. Some others can use electricity. But, until the oil-wells were discovered, wood was the only fuel in the country. So where trees were able to grow faster than goats could eat them, many millions were cut down and not replaced.

Even now, there are large parts of the country where that is still going on, and it has been going on for many thousands of years. People were living in Iran long before the Iranians came there. So before we look more closely at Iran today, let us find out what we can about the peoples of its past.

The Medes and the Persians

If the Bible story of Noah and his ark tells of something that really happened, Iran must have been the country where Noah made his home after the ark came to rest on Mount Ararat. Mount Ararat now belongs to Iran's north-western neighbour Turkey, but it is naturally connected with the Elburz and Zagros Ranges of Iran. So, when Noah brought his family and his animals down from the mountain, he was moving into what is now an Iranian province called Azarbaijan. And it is not surprising that he decided to settle there and plant grape-vines. Azarbaijan has better soil and a higher rainfall than the rest of upland Iran, and so is the most fertile part of the whole country, except for the lowlands near the Caspian Sea.

Perhaps this prehistoric Iranian metal sculpture suggests that the first tame goats may have been bred in this area

A new dam which has been built in the region of Mount Ararat

Of course, we have nothing to prove that the story did happen as it is told in the Bible, or even that it happened at all. The fact is, however, that north-west Iran was one of the first places where people are known to have lived as settled farmers. In many parts of what is now called the Middle East, later people believed that these farmers were their ancestors. They also believed that wine was invented in north-west Iran, and that the first tame goats had been bred there. And they must have wondered why their wine-making, goat-breeding ancestors had lived in such a high, wild, distant place—until a storyteller gave them an answer. Perhaps after watching the Karun or some other lowland river burst its banks, he told them that their ancestors had fled from the lowlands to the highlands to escape a much more serious flood—a flood that put the whole of the lowlands deep under water.

He may well have been partly right. Some archaeologists say that there was a deep and disastrous flood over the lowlands about six thousand years ago, and survivors could have reached Mount Ararat. However they may have arrived, people were settled in north-west Iran around 4000 B.C., and perhaps earlier. They grew grapes and grain, and bred both sheep and goats. They may also have mined copper. At that time, some of the more advanced peoples were using copper instead of stone for their tools and weapons. And there are copper deposits in many parts of upland Iran.

That is all we know, or can guess, about the people of the Noah's Ark story, and we know very little more about other peoples who came to upland Iran during the next two thousand years. But then there came a people about whom we know a great deal. They were nomads from beyond Mount Ararat— wandering tribes who rode horses, drove cattle and carried their household goods in horse-drawn wooden waggons. As far as we know, these nomads were the first people in the world to move vehicles by horse-power, and perhaps the first to use vehicles with wheels. They were also the first true Iranians.

We call them the first *true* Iranians because they gave the country its name Iran, after their own name Irani, or Aryans. They came from a very much larger group of fair-skinned nomadic tribes which had been spreading from the lands west of the Caspian Sea into several parts of Asia and also into Europe. Nowadays, we call the whole group the Indo-Europeans, because their language was the ancestor of nearly every language now spoken in Europe, and of many languages now spoken in India and countries near India—including, of course, Iran. Over thousands of years, all those languages have become very different from each other. But we can see how they are related if we compare some common words in any two of them. For instance, where an English-speaker says *mother, name, mouse* and *two*, an Iranian says *madar, nam, mush* and *do*.

Of the several Aryan tribes who moved on to the uplands, the names of two became famous: the Medes, and the Parsa or Persians. In time, the Medes and the Persians took over the whole upland area. They turned it into two strong kingdoms where most of the people lived settled, civilised lives under laws that were very strict, but also very fair.

Persepolis – relief of Parsa soldiers carved in about 500 BC

"The law of the Medes and Persians" is mentioned in the Bible story of Daniel. Although Daniel was a captive from the country that is now Israel, he had become a very important man among the Persians, and a friend of the Persian king. But he was still condemned to die in a lion's den after his enemies had caused him to break the law. Even his friend King Darius could not change the law to save him. So, when he came out of the den unharmed, the Persians took it as a sign that his God had soothed the lions, and they began to think of him as a holy man. Modern Iranians also think of him as a holy man, and show visitors a very old tomb which they say is his.

The tomb is in the lowland oil-well area, near what is left of an ancient city named Susa. Susa was once the capital of a country whose people were not Indo-Europeans like the Medes and the Persians. They were subjects of the powerful Assyrian Empire which also wanted to rule Iran. But the Medes came down from the uplands and conquered them. And when the Persian king Cyrus conquered the Medes and became king of all Iran, in about 550 B.C., he made Susa his own capital.

From Susa, Cyrus began the great Persian Empire by taking nearly every country that had been part of the Assyrian Empire, and every other country between Iran and the Mediterranean and Aegean Seas. For the people of those countries, the change was a welcome one. Their old rulers had often been harsh and merciless; from Cyrus they had

The monument
erected over the tomb
of Daniel at Susa

mercy and generosity. Perhaps the people who had most
cause to thank him were the Jews, who had been treated very
harshly indeed. Not only did he free a great many Jews who
had been held captive in Babylonia (now Iraq) for fifty years
and more. He also helped them to re-settle in their homeland
and rebuild their famous temple in Jerusalem, which the
Babylonians had destroyed.

When Cyrus died, his son Cambyses added some of north
Africa to the new empire. But Cambyses did not live long.
After his death, seven of his relatives all claimed the right
to be the new shahanshah, as the rulers of the empire came

to be called. *Shahanshah* means *King of kings*, and the later kings of Iran all used that title, though they usually shortened it to shah.

With seven rivals wanting to be king of kings, the empire could easily have broken up in civil war. However, an old Iranian story says that they wisely decided to settle the question among themselves, in a peaceful and very unusual way. They would race their horses against each other, and the empire would go to the man who rode the winner. It was also a very unusual horse race: so that every rival would have the fairest possible chance, the winner was not to be the first horse past the winning-post, but the first horse to neigh after all had passed the winning-post.

We do not know how true that story is. Perhaps the only truth in it is that the civilised, empire-building Iranians still kept their old nomadic love of horsemanship. But we do know that somehow the new shahanshah was chosen peacefully. His name was Daryusha—or, as he is called in the Bible and most history books, Darius.

As he had beaten his rivals peacefully, so Darius began his reign peacefully. Instead of trying to enlarge his empire, he made a better empire of what he had. For many centuries after he died, he was best remembered for finishing a great system of roads that Cyrus had begun. The main road, known as the Royal Road, ran for nearly 3,200 kilometres (2,000 miles) through the heart of the empire, from Susa to the shores of the Aegean Sea, opposite Greece. Other roads branched off into every province of the empire. This network of highways made old Iran a great trading centre, a channel through which all the land trade between eastern and western Asia had to pass. Even today, much of the motor traffic in the Middle East moves on highways built over or close to the roads that Darius made.

Darius himself also found a very important use for his road system when at last he began massing soldiers to enlarge the empire. His aim was to move into Europe by conquering Greece. By the year 492 B.C., he had gathered a huge army at the western end of the Royal Road, with enough ships to carry them across to Greece. They had hardly set sail when a tremendous storm wrecked the whole fleet. Most of the men were saved, but all their equipment was lost. Two busy years passed before Darius could try again. This time the army landed safely in Greece, 40 kilometres (25 miles) from the city of Athens. There, they met a much smaller Greek force and were driven back to the sea after one fierce battle. The name of the battlefield was Marathon. (We call the long-distance race in the Olympic Games the Marathon in honour of a Greek athlete who was killed by the effort of running back to Athens with the news that the army of Darius had been beaten.)

Even Marathon was not enough for Darius. He began at once to mass an even bigger army which his son Xerxes took over, since Darius died before it was ready. The army that Xerxes led to Greece was the biggest that the world had then seen. It numbered 400,000 men, from Iran itself and from every far fringe of the empire. There were even huge black warriors from the African lands south of Egypt, which were then thought to be on the southern edge of the world. Naturally enough, the Greeks wanted to know what was coming against them. So they sent spies across to Asia. The spies were captured and they expected the Persians to kill them. But Xerxes let them see the whole of his mighty army, and then sent them back to Greece, hoping that their reports would terrify their countrymen.

The Greeks were worried but not weakened. The Persians were more confident than ever. Where the Aegean Sea narrows down to a strait called the Hellespont, they tied a line of boats from shore to shore and used it as a bridge into Greece. After failing to stop them in a famous battle at the Pass of Thermopylae, the Greeks let them march down the coast as far as Athens, while eight hundred Persian warships sailed abreast of them. But then the Greeks struck back. As Xerxes sat watching from a seaside hill, a Greek fleet destroyed his ships. And, in a land battle near Athens, Greek soldiers turned his huge army back to Asia. The Persian Empire had spread as far as it could go.

Xerxes was the last of the great empire-building shahs. Those who came after him could barely hold the empire together, much less make it bigger. One of them spent the first years of his reign at war with a rebel brother, who even brought in ten thousand Greek mercenary soldiers to help him. When the rebel was killed, these mercenaries had to struggle home across half the empire. Their leader—a man named Xenophon—described the journey in a book which is still one of the best true adventure stories ever written.

Seventy years later, in 331 B.C., there were more Greek soldiers in the heart of the Persian Empire, but these were helping neither the shah nor a rebel. They had come to help themselves. Allied with their northern neighbours the Macedonians, and led by the young Macedonian king Alexander, they were an army of invaders set on making Alexander the ruler of a world empire. They defeated a Persian army 500,000 strong, which used elephants in the same way as armies of our own century use tanks. They destroyed Persepolis, the magnificent capital city which Darius had built on the uplands of Iran, to replace lowland

The Gate of Xerxes at Persepolis

The central palace staircase at Persepolis which gives some idea of the splendour of the ancient city

Susa. They marched across the Hindu Kush Mountains to the great plains of northern India. And when they returned to Iran, Alexander began to call himself the shahanshah. The real shahanshah had died, leaving no Iranian strong enough to challenge the invaders.

Instead of turning the empire of the Medes and Persians into a world empire, Alexander had begun its end. Only a year after he came back from India he died of malaria, a fever that can still be caught in some parts of Iran and the countries near by. None of his generals would accept any of the others as leader. So they divided the empire, each making himself king of a separate part.

Although it is more than 2,300 years since Alexander marched through Iran, Iranians still feel close to their ancient empire. They also feel very proud of the men who made the empire—not only because these men were such mighty conquerors, but also because they were usually kind and generous to the conquered peoples, and made the conquered countries better places to live in. That was something to notice in the ancient world, where human life and living conditions often meant much less than they do under the most brutal governments of our own time. The advanced and democratic ancient Greeks thought of the Persians as their worst enemies, but even they praised the behaviour and the government of Persian rulers like Cyrus the Great.

The behaviour of the Persians came partly from customs that went back to their early nomadic life outside Iran, and partly from an idea of their great religious teacher Zoroaster. Zoroaster was born in Iran long before the Persian Empire began. He grew up to become a farmer and a thinker—a thinker who came to an idea that was strange to every nation of his time except the Jews. It was the idea of a God who cared about the behaviour of human beings; who wanted them to do good and fight evil. From that idea came a religion which most Iranians followed for nearly one thousand years after their empire fell, and which some Iranians still follow.

The religion of Zoroaster also helped to shape the Jewish and Christian religions which gave many peoples of the modern world their main patterns for civilised behaviour.

And in one small way—perhaps without knowing it—Christians are still linked with Zoroaster, through the story of the first Christmas. Nowadays, the three wise men who came from the east to find the baby Jesus are usually thought of as kings. But they are also called the magi, and the first Christians knew that magi were priests of Zoroaster's religion, famous everywhere for their wisdom and for their interest in studying the stars. That is why the Christmas story says that the three wise men found their way to Bethlehem by following a star, and why we should imagine them not as kings, but as priests of ancient Iran.

Because magi were so widely known as wise men, some people in the ancient world were inclined also to think of them as wizards, men who could work wonders beyond the power of ordinary human beings. So they invented a new word for such wonders, and the word is still used in many languages. When we say that something is done by *magic*, we are really suggesting that it could be done only by someone who knew what the magi knew. But we owe the magi more than an everyday word. We also owe them a very important science, because they were perhaps the first people to make a serious study of the stars, and certainly the first to pass their knowledge on. What they believed about the stars was not always right, but it was enough to show the way into the science of astronomy, which in our own time has discovered more about the stars than the magi could have dreamed, and which may one day help us to reach them.

Unhappily, as the magi became more and more interested in their studies, they lost interest in their other work of helping people to understand and follow the teaching of Zoroaster. So the people began to lose interest in the magi, and to think of finding a new religion. They had no real need to do that; in A.D. 641, a new religion found them.

Islam to Oil-wells

After Alexander's generals had divided the old empire, they could not hold all that they had taken. Iran fell to another invader, and then became independent again, under its own shahs. It was not easy to remain independent. Over the centuries, much of the old empire fell to two growing European powers, first the Romans, and then the Greeks of Byzantium. Both wanted to take Iran as well, and tried hard to do so. But the Iranians managed to keep them away. They even defeated a Roman army, and took a Roman emperor prisoner.

Later, when they were attacked by the Byzantine Greeks, it seemed likely that they might make another Persian Empire. They pushed the Greeks back along the whole length of the old Royal Road to the shores of the Aegean Sea, where Cyrus,

Darius and Xerxes had massed their armies more than a thousand years before. There, the Greeks made a stand, and stopped them. But it was not the power of Byzantine Greece that ended the chance of another Persian Empire. It was a fresh invasion of Iran from a very unlikely place—Arabia.

Until then, Arabia had played only a very small part in the affairs of the outside world. But in about A.D. 616 an Arab named Muhammad began to preach a new religion which many of his countrymen accepted with great enthusiasm. Muhammad gave his religion the name Islam, an Arabic word which means "giving in to the will of God". The God of Islam was the God of the Jewish and Christian religions. In fact, Muhammad drew much of his teachings from the Bible. But he and his early followers also had many ideas

The mosque is the Muslim Place of worship. Many of them, like this one in Isfahan, are large and beautifully decorated

that are not found in the Bible—including the idea that the best way to make Islam a world religion was to conquer the world. So great was their enthusiasm that they did conquer many countries. Armies of Arabs swept through north Africa, into parts of Europe, and over much of western Asia.

In A.D. 641 they conquered Iran. Iran became a Muslim country—that is, a country accepting Islam as its state religion. Having been conquered, the Iranians had very little choice. But as many had become dissatisfied with their old religion, only a few were unhappy with the change. Most of them have been Muslims ever since.

With the change in religion came other changes. Though it kept its own shahs for most of the time, Iran was now part of an Arab empire controlled by the Caliph, the head of the Muslim religion. When the Caliph chose Baghdad in neighbouring Iraq as his capital city, he also became the real ruler of Iran. Under Muslim rule, education and law were based

The main building of Tehran's first university. The writing over the entrance is in the Arabic alphabet which is the ordinary alphabet of Iran

on the Koran, the Muslim holy book. And the Koran could be studied only in the Arabic language. So educated Iranians had to learn and use the Arabic language as well as their own. This changed their own language by bringing many Arabic words into it. They also began to write their own language in the Arabic alphabet, which is still the ordinary alphabet of Iran.

More changes came in their traditional habits and amusements, their daily work and even their food and drink. For example, they lived in the country where wine was probably invented, and they had always been wine-drinkers, but now—because of a strict Muslim rule—they could drink no wine at all. Muslim farmers who grew grapes had to dry them to make raisins, or use their juice to make a sweet, non-alcoholic drink called *doshab*.

There were changes in the people themselves, too. Arab settlers followed the Arab army, mainly to the lowlands near the Persian Gulf, but also to parts of the uplands. Many of these Arabs lived in separate communities, as the Arabs of Khuzestan do now. But there was still enough mixing of peoples to give some modern Iranians an appearance that is as much Arabic as it is Indo-European.

Most Iranians settled to their new way of life fairly easily, but it was too much for some. Shortly after the Arab invasion, a large group of them left Iran for ever. They settled as a separate community on the west coast of India, and about 100,000 of their descendants are still there. Called the Parsees, they speak a form of the Iranian language, and follow the religion of Zoroaster—which may explain why they are very well-known for giving help to the poor and distressed.

The changes under the rule of the Arab caliphs were not all on the Iranian side. Iran changed the Arabs, too. At that time, the Arabs were fairly backward in the arts, crafts and sciences, whereas the Iranians were well in advance of most other peoples. They passed their knowledge and skills on to the Arab invaders who, in turn, passed them to the rest of the Muslim world. Later, travellers from Britain and other developing Christian countries brought some of the same knowledge home with them. For that reason, some people are now inclined to say that modern European culture owes a great debt to the Arabs. However, it would be much more true to say that both Europeans and Arabs owe a great debt to the non-Arab culture of old Iran.

For instance, the famous book called in English *The Arabian Nights Entertainments* originally had nothing to do with Arabia. It was a set of old Iranian stories which came to Europe through the Arab countries. In the same way, we hear that Arabs invented a navigation instrument used by exploring seafarers such as Christopher Columbus; that they set the styles of architecture which gave the Muslim world some of the most beautiful buildings ever made; that they developed the branch of mathematics called algebra; that they wrote the text-books used in every European medical school during the Middle Ages. But all those things—and many more now often credited to Arabs—were in fact done by Iranians.

Through their religious leaders, the Iranians also caused a very wide break in Islam—a break as serious as the one which later divided western Christians into Roman Catholics and Protestants. In Islam, the two opposing groups were called Sunni Muslims and Shi'a Muslims, and it was among the Iranians that the Shi'a group began. On the other hand, the Arab caliphs and their followers led the Sunni group.

The first result of the break was that the Iranians gradually became independent of the Arabs, although this was not achieved wholly by their own efforts, nor wholly in a way that pleased them. After A.D. 1037, Iran and its neighbours were invaded by three different warlike peoples from central Asia. These invasions were spread over four hundred years, and one of them—by Mongols—was particularly brutal and destructive. The Mongols set out to destroy every sign of civilisation—books, buildings, vineyards and gardens, even the irrigation systems which kept the food crops alive. Among the wreckage was Baghdad, the city of the Sunni caliphs; the caliphs never ruled again in this part of the Muslim world. When the last invasion was over, Iran rebuilt itself into the fully independent country which it has been nearly ever since.

The second result of the break was that Iran became an enemy of its north-western neighbour Turkey. Many of the first waves of central Asian invaders were nomads called Turks. They spread into what became Turkey, captured it from the Byzantine Greeks, and began to build a wide-spreading empire which was to last into our own century.

Like the Iranians, the Turks had become Muslims. But they were Sunni Muslims. Indeed their sultans (emperors) were also the caliphs from about 1514 to 1924. And so they could not persuade the Shi'a Iranians to join their empire. Besides, the Iranians were determined to hold their independence. For the next three hundred years, they were almost continually fighting border wars against the Turks; the fighting stopped only when both nations found that they were in danger from their northern neighbour Russia.

Even during the Mongol invasions, Iran had remained the great trading channel between eastern and western Asia, and so between eastern Asia and Europe. But when the Turkish Empire spread right to the borders of Iran, the channel was partly blocked. Also, many European countries were themselves not very friendly to the Turks, and their traders preferred to avoid Turkish territory. This led them to think of making a sea-link with Iran through the Persian Gulf. Early in the seventeenth century, Portuguese, Dutch, French and British traders began to arrive in the Gulf ports. The British were the most successful. They were allowed to have a permanent trading-station at Bandar Abbas, newly named after the great Shah Abbas I, who had given them the right to be there.

This trading-station was not the first link between Iran and

Britain. Traders and other British visitors had come and gone in previous centuries. An English Christian monk, St. Willibald, visited Iran as far back as A.D. 722. There may also have been an even earlier link with England. England has two towns with the name St. Ives, one in Cornwall, and one in the part of Cambridgeshire called Huntingdon. The town in Cornwall seems to have taken its name from a saintly Irish princess, but the saint who gave his name to the Huntingdon town was a bishop who helped convert the English to Christianity, and he probably came from Iran. However, all of those were only occasional links. The trading-station at Bandar Abbas began a lasting friendly connection between Iran and Britain. Apart from a few unhappy breaks, this lasted from the

Modern Isfahan boasts many new buildings. This picture shows the library in a new school

days of Shah Abbas I into the reign of the last Shah, Mohammed Reza Pahlavi, who left the country after republican rioting in 1979.

Under Shah Abbas, Iran won back the prosperity and greatness it had lost during the Mongol invasions. This can be judged today by a visit to Isfahan, Shah Abbas' magnificent capital city. During its long history, Iran has almost certainly had more capital cities than any other country. Even in the last five hundred years there have been seven. But none of the other six (nor any of earlier times) has equalled Isfahan. That is why, since the reign of Shah Abbas, Iranians have had the saying: "Isfahan is half the world". There is also another saying, taken from an old Iranian poem, which goes: "Everything would be fine in Isfahan—if it had no people". But that was meant as a joke against the citizens, who were perhaps too much inclined to boast about their city.

Shah Abbas belonged to a line of shahs called the Safavis, whose family home was in north-west Iran. The first Safavi shah had chosen Tabriz, the chief city of that area, as his

The palace of Shah Abbas in Isfahan

capital. But Tabriz was dangerously close to Turkey. Also, many of the people in the north-west seemed unreliable. They were Turks—and even Mongols—who had stayed there after the invasions. So the next Safavi shah moved to Qasvin, much further from the Turkish border. When even Qasvin seemed too close to Turkey, Shah Abbas made a capital of Isfahan, midway between the Caspian Sea and the Persian Gulf.

The Safavi shah who came after him kept Isfahan as the capital. It remained the capital until 1722, when the last Safavi lost it to invaders from Afghanistan, on the eastern side of Iran. He also very nearly lost the whole country, as Russians and Turks were attacking at the same time. However, a very great soldier—himself descended from a Turkish invader—beat back all three enemies, and then blocked a possible fourth by marching his army into India. From there, he took to Iran the famous jewelled peacock throne on which Indian emperors had been crowned, and on which the shahs of Iran were crowned ever afterwards. It was too late for him to make himself the first shah to be crowned on it. Before he went to India he had already become Shah Nadir, by taking the crown from the last Safavi.

Isfahan had suffered badly while the Afghans held it, and so Shah Nadir changed the capital to Mashad, near his birthplace in the north-east. But another change came after fifty years or so. In about 1785, Shah Agha Mohammed moved to a city nearer his own birthplace. The city was Tehran, which is still the capital of Iran.

Throughout the nineteenth and early twentieth centuries, there were no shahs so strong or so successful as Abbas I and Nadir. Some were so weak that they lost valuable parts of northern Iran permanently to Russia. These losses were not liked by the people. Nor were the facts that the country was growing poorer and poorer, and that the shahs were being controlled more and more by both the British and the Russian governments. But the wishes and opinions of the people had very little consideration from the shahs. The shahs were despots—men who ruled alone and allowed no interference from anyone except the country's religious leaders, or sometimes from powerful foreigners who could provide them with extra money and protect them from their rivals. So, although the Iranians had always been a democratic people in their daily lives, there was no democracy in their government.

However, as Iran's connections with European countries grew closer, the people began to learn more about life in Europe. That led them to ask for a government, laws, civil rights and services like those in such countries as Britain and France. By the early 1900s, they were asking so strongly that Shah Muzaffar-ed-Din was forced to promise that he would rule through an elected parliament.

The parliament, called the *Majlis*, was at first a very weak one. The shahs found that they need not take it too seriously, and it had hardly begun to act when some news from Khuzestan made the country even more attractive to foreigners. The news was that oil had been discovered—enough oil

The Senate, Tehran. This is the upper house of the Iranian parliament

to make Iran one of the world's greatest suppliers. Shortly afterwards, the First World War began. Partly because of the oil, Iran was occupied by the British and the Russians. And when the war ended it seemed that one or both of them might take over the government. The country was in such a poor and rebellious state that neither the Shah nor the Majlis could put it in order.

However—as in the time of Nadir—a soldier came to the rescue. He was Reza Khan Pahlavi, the commander of a division of mounted troops who had been trying to defend the northern borders. Reza Khan wanted neither the British nor the Russians in control of the government. But of the two he prefered the British. When he heard that the British were not going to stay, he led some of his troops to Tehran. There, he took over the government, and forced the Shah to make him commander-in-chief of the army. Later, in 1923, he became prime minister. Then, in 1925, he had the Shah deposed and put himself on the peacock throne.

45

Reza was Shah of Iran for the next sixteen years. He succeeded not only in putting the country in order, but also in making it independent again. His government then set out on a policy of making Iran more up-to-date, mainly by taking away the powers of the Muslim religious leaders. That does not mean that either the Shah or the government was against the Muslim religion. But for many centuries Muslim leaders had interfered in government, influenced the law, controlled education and kept the people clinging to many ideas and customs which had begun to seem backward and unjust. One such custom was that women had always to cover their faces with a large veil when they were out of their houses. Now, Shah Reza made it illegal for them to do so. Rather surprisingly, many women were not at all pleased.

The tomb of Shah Reza, Tehran

It was another world war that ended the reign of Shah Reza —the Second World War, which began in 1939. Remembering the years of the First World War, the Shah's government declared that Iran would favour neither side. But the Shah himself seemed to favour the Germans; and when Germany tried to use Iran as a base, the British and the Russians moved in. Many Iranians approved of this, and the Shah decided that he would rather not rule a country occupied against his will. In 1941, he gave up the throne to his son Mohammed Reza Pahlavi, whose long reign was to be the last before Iran became a republic.

Shah and Ayatollah

In many western countries, most of the people live and work in cities and large industrial towns. But the pattern of life is different in Iran. There, hardly more than one third of the forty-one million people are city-dwellers. The others— nearly twenty-seven million of them—are village people and nomads who live mainly by growing crops and grazing animals.

During the 1960s these farming millions took part in a

revolution—but not a revolution against the government. This was a revolution begun by the Shah himself. Its aim was to achieve a higher standard of living for both town and country people. It was called the White Revolution because it set about achieving its changes peacefully.

For farmers, the most welcome change was that very many of them became the owners of the land that they farmed, and so got a better return from their work. Before the White Revolution, the return was small indeed, often as little as one fifth of the produce of one or two fields, which left the farmer with hardly anything to sell after he had fed himself and his family.

This happened because nearly all the farmland in Iran was owned by a fairly small number of people who were not farmers—nor even country people—themselves. They lived in the cities or abroad, and expected the profits from their land to keep them there in comfort.

A landlord of this kind owned all the land worked by the farmers of a village, or perhaps a group of villages. The farmers who used the land did not give him rent in money. Instead, at harvest times, his agent took one fifth of every crop. And it was a lucky farmer who had to give only that. Landlords very often owned the qanats which watered the fields, and the farmers had to give another one fifth of their crops for the right to use the water. The farmers also needed ploughs and other tools, a donkey and often an ox for the heavier work, and seed for new crops. But they rarely had the money to buy such things. So the landlord's agent provided them, and took one fifth of the crops in payment for the seeds, and another one fifth in payment for the use of the tools and the animals.

All those fifths for the landlord left the farmer to manage as best he could with only one fifth of what he grew. Shah Mohammed Reza began the White Revolution because farmers were finding it harder and harder to manage. He began it by setting an example. The farmlands of nearly three thousand villages were royal lands, which passed from shah to shah. So the Shah himself was the biggest landlord in the country. To start the White Revolution he offered to sell some of his lands to the farmers who worked them. They were not asked to buy at once. All they had to do was sell the fifths of crops that had previously gone to the Shah, and give the government bank a small part of the money every year until the whole price of the land was paid.

The first sales were a small experiment, but the farmers seemed to like the idea. So the Shah sold more of his lands. Then the government decided to buy farms from other big landowners, and sell those to farmers in the same way. After ten years or so, there were very few farmers who still had to set aside four fifths of their crops for other people. But it seems that the White Revolution did not manage to make every farmer his own landlord. In order to get ready money, some farmers began selling their land to new landlords, and then paying rent for it.

A farm donkey

There were problems at first. Through their agents, the landlords had helped the farmers in many ways. For instance, they kept the irrigation systems working, and they chose seed that was right for the soil and the climate. And the farmers sometimes made mistakes when they tried to do such things for themselves. But the White Revolution covered that, too. Specially trained helpers went to the villages and worked with the farmers who needed them. The helpers also taught farmers how to improve and protect their land and their crops, how to use modern equipment, and how to replace the old qanats with water pipes in districts where the government has built dams for water storage. Because of all that, Iran now has much more land under crops than it had before the White Revolution. It also has bigger and better harvests, as well as farmers who get a fairer return for the harvests.

50

Even so, most farms are small, and for village people the standard of living is usually very simple. In many villages, most of the houses have only one room. Few houses in any village have more than two rooms, with perhaps a kind of cellar dug below them, as a cool living-room for the summer. However, not much space is taken up by furniture. For meals, people usually sit round a cloth spread on the floor, often over a carpet woven by the women and children of the village, with wool from the village sheep. They sleep on the floor, too,

Modern equipment and machinery is now being used, as can be seen here, on farms and building-sites in Iran

An Iranian farmer among his peach trees

using bedding which is rolled up during the day, to make more room. In very cold weather—and it can be bitterly cold on the uplands and in the mountains—the bedding is arranged like the spokes of a wheel, round a slow-burning charcoal fire. Then a big woollen quilt is rigged like a low tent over fire and bedding, and the sleepers lie under it, with only their heads showing.

Naturally enough, they are under the quilt with their toes to the charcoal very early in the evening. There is no other way to keep warm. They go to bed early in other seasons, too—perhaps up on the flat roof under the stars when the nights are hot. They go to bed early partly because farm work starts with daylight, but also because there is little else to do after dark. Electricity has not yet come to many villages; and when it does come very few people have uses for it at night. Many people cannot read, and there are no village libraries for those who can read. The television service cannot reach many of the villages, nor could the people afford television sets if they did. Most still find it hard to afford even a battery radio. However—as part of the White Revolution—some rural areas were given community centres in places which village people can visit fairly easily. These have both radio and television sets, as well as films shown by travelling cinemas, and even occasional "live" plays and concerts.

In the villages themselves, a visit from a travelling story-teller is usually the only entertainment open to everyone. If a storyteller comes during the month which Muslims call Moharram, he tells of a great battle which was fought on the tenth day of that month, about 1,300 years ago, and led to the break between Shi'a Muslims and Sunni Muslims. If he comes in another month, he tells mainly of other battles in the distant past, and the adventures of ancient Iranian heroes. Perhaps the most popular of these stories, about two warriors named Sohrab and Rustem, has been retold as a poem in English, and is sometimes printed in the school books of English-speaking countries.

In Iran, the story is also told as a poem. So are many of the other tales told by storytellers. The Iranians have always been fond of poetry. They are very proud of such great poets as Firdawsi, who told the whole story of early Iran in a very long poem called *Shahnama*, which means "The Book of Kings". Another favourite poet was Omar Khayyam, whose verses are also popular in English. Omar must have been a very busy man. Besides writing poetry, founding a school of astronomy, giving Iran a more accurate calendar and helping to develop algebra, he is said to have followed the trade of tentmaking.

When the storyteller has left a village, the people must make their own entertainment until he comes again. But then they are used to making do without much help from outside. There may well be no shop in the village. If there is a shop, its stock is small and simple—mainly paraffin for lamps and perhaps small cooking-stoves; rice, sugar, tea and salt; tobacco and matches; thread, needles and cotton cloth to make clothes. Village people can manage with those things and little else apart from what they grow or gather. Often they can manage without the cotton cloth, for the women of the village spin and weave their own, from cotton grown by the men.

Apart from houses and a small shop, there are only two other buildings likely to be found in most villages. They are a mosque and a bath-house. The Iranians like to be clean, and village people need the bath-house because their own homes have neither bathrooms nor running water. Bathhouses are built underground. Each has at least two pools of water—one hot and one cold—and these are looked after by a man whose job is to keep the hot pool hot and both pools clean. Where there are plenty of trees, he uses wood-fires to heat the water. Where trees are scarce—and that is nearly everywhere in the uplands—he burns dried dung. He is usually paid for his work by the people who use the bath-house—more often with something that he can eat rather than with money.

Bath-houses are for people only. Running through every village there is either a natural stream or an open water channel connecting with a qanat, and the women do their household washing in those. Open water channels are still used in some cities and large towns, too. Under city conditions, they can be very unhealthy, so more and more of them are now being replaced by piped water.

The other building likely to be found in most villages —the mosque—is a Muslim church. Until recently, the mosque was also the village school, and its minister (called the *mullah*) was the teacher. No girls went to it, and most of the boys went for only a short time. Some did not go at all. From the mullah, the pupils learnt a little reading and writing, and some lessons from the Koran, but that was all.

However, many villages now have a school apart from the mosque. Girls as well as boys go to this one. In fact, the law says that they must go to it for five years, although many still leave after a shorter time, and some manage to avoid going at all. These may number as many as twenty per cent of the country's school-age children.

In spite of the new village schools, the mullah of the village mosque still has some teaching to do. Good Muslims must understand the Koran and also learn some of it by heart, and most village parents want their children to become good Muslims. In fact, it is now almost compulsory for Iranians to be good Muslims—or at any rate to be sure that they do not break any of the rules and laws of Islam, the Muslim religion. That is because Iran is no longer a kingdom, but an Islamic republic whose president and parliament are under the authority of a Muslim religious leader, and whose decisions must all be approved by a Muslim council under the control of that leader. At present, the leader is the head of the Shi'a Muslims, the Ayatollah Ruhollah Khomeini.

This change happened in 1979. In spite of the White Revolution and other reforms planned for the nation's benefit, Shah Mohammed Reza grew less and less popular as his reign went on. There were many reasons for the unpopularity, but the main one was a quarrel with the Muslim religious leaders. Like his father, Shah Mohammed Reza would not allow the Muslim leaders to interfere in government, influence the law and attempt to control the people's lives as they had done in the past—and when the religious leaders resisted, he sent the Ayatollah Khomeini into exile.

Unfortunately for the Shah, he misjudged the people's feelings for their faith, and their loyalty to him. During 1978, there were large and often violent demonstrations against him throughout the country, and by early 1979 it was clear that he could not raise enough support to hold his throne. He and his family left the country, and the Ayatollah returned amid great rejoicing, as well as a good deal of revengeful violence and bloodshed. Within a few weeks a majority of Iranians declared, by referendum, that their country was to be an Islamic republic.

In the following year a new *Majlis* (parliament) was elected, and one of the first matters to come before it was a serious dispute between Iran and its neighbour Iraq over their rights to part of a strip of waterway called the Shatt al Arab. Talk did not settle this dispute; and, in September 1980, Iraqi forces invaded Iran.

At first, the Iraqis seemed to have the upper hand. They occupied part of Iran, and beat off all attempts to remove them until June 1982. Then, after a hard fought battle near the city of Khorramshahr, the Iranians forced them to retreat into their own country. However, the war still continued.

Partly because of this war, and partly because of many major changes still being made by the new government, it is at present very difficult to find out exactly what is happening throughout Iran. However, where the war permits it, work seems to be going on in much the same way as it did under the Shah, although daily life is affected by the strict enforcement of the rules and laws of Islam. There seems to be no doubt that people who break these rules and laws are treated severely—and such treatment can be very severe indeed. There are no less than 109 offences which judges may punish with the death penalty.

Many people in Iran today still cannot read and write. In the foreground of this picture is the desk of a public letter-writer

One group of people who are certainly receiving severe treatment are the members of a fairly new religion called Bahai. Bahai was started in Iran about 120 years ago, by some Shi'a Muslims who were no longer satisfied with Islam. At first, the Bahais were cruelly persecuted. Some were even killed. And although they were treated a little more tolerantly as the years went by, persecution has recently begun again. The Bahais in Iran are not helped by the fact that their religion has its world centre in Israel, and many followers in the U.S.A. Republican Iran is not at all friendly to either of those countries.

Fortunately, Bahais do not attract much attention to themselves, as they have no special buildings for religious meetings. They meet quietly in private houses. And most Iranian Bahais live in the towns, where houses are often much bigger than village houses. Many houses too are shut in by high walls of yellowish brick, so that neither the garden nor much of the house can be seen from the street. That is the traditional way of building a town house in Iran, but some of the newer houses follow the more open western styles. Also—especially in Tehran—many townspeople have begun to live in large blocks of flats which look no different from modern high-rise buildings in other parts of the world.

Of course there are small houses in the towns, too. Indeed, most townspeople have no more living-space than village people. Their houses are very much like the mud-brick village houses, but crowded along alleyways and narrow, winding streets. Mainly in Tehran, there are also some people with no houses at all. These are people who have moved in from the country hoping for better-paid work in new factory industries, or simply because there was no longer any work for them in the country. Most of them do find work, because Iran's factory industries are growing very quickly. But houses to suit the rent they can afford are very scarce. So they gather any old rubbish that will make four walls and a roof, and build little shacks for themselves on empty ground. The government cannot very well move them, because it has said that it wants less people in the villages and more people working in town industries.

It is not only the hope of work that attracts these people away from the villages. It is also the entertainments that a city can offer—including chances to play and watch games

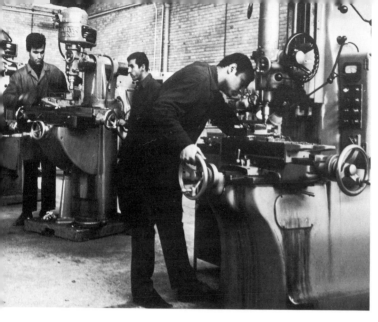

regularly. Indoor and outdoor games have always been popular in Iran. Indeed, at least two games which are now international were invented there. They are polo and chess —and players of both games anywhere still use some old Iranian words in disguise. For instance, a polo-player calls a round of his game a *chukker*; and when a chess-player says "Checkmate" he is really saying the Iranian words "*Shah mat*", which mean "The king is dead".

Polo could hardly be called an Iranian game nowadays. The national sport is wrestling, and next to that Iranians like ball-games from western countries—especially football. But they still play indoor games like chess, both at home and in kafekhanas. The word *kafekhana* means coffee-house. But very few kafekhanas serve coffee now. Most Iranians gave up coffee in favour of tea a long time ago. And it is tea that the customers drink as they sit on the carpet-covered benches of kafekhanas, puffing in turn at a "hubble-bubble" pipe, and perhaps playing games or listening to a storyteller.

The customers are nearly always men. Women are not allowed in most kafekhanas. Even at home, Muslim women are supposed to keep out of the way when their men are drinking tea or having a meal with visitors. Nowadays, the rule is often broken. But many women still obey it. They also veil their faces if the visitor should happen to see them. Shah Reza's law forbidding women to wear the veil was not very successful. So many people preferred the old custom that the law has been put aside. A woman may now veil herself or not as she—or perhaps her husband—wishes. Incidentally, the veil in Iran is really a large shawl. Called a *chadur*, it covers the whole body except the hands and feet; in very strict Muslim families girls start wearing it as early as their sixth birthday.

A scene in a gymnasium which specialises in traditional exercises and games. The "Indian" clubs in the background have been used in Iran since ancient times

A girl wearing a chadur which is really like a large shawl

The traditional colour for a chadur is black but many women wear brightly-coloured patterned ones, especially when they are at home.

Veiled or not, Iranian women now have much more freedom than they did in the past. They also have equal rights with men in some important ways. For instance, they can vote at elections for the Majlis, which is a parliament of 268 members democratically elected every four years by all citizens aged at least twenty. There are equal opportunities in education, too. Primary schools, secondary schools and universities are open to girls as well as to boys. But girls—and boys too—from farming villages often find it hard to get more than a primary education. The villages have no secondary schools, and farming people are often unable—or unwilling—to send their childern to secondary schools in the towns.

It is not only the farming parents who may be unwilling to let their children have a secondary education. There are also some town parents who like their children to leave school at an early age—sometimes even before they have finished their five years in primary school. These parents are usually unemployed, or working for very low wages, and they need the little extra money that a child can earn.

Such children usually do fine and delicate work in traditional craft industries, especially carpet-making. The intricate designs of Persian carpets are made by knotting short pieces of coloured wool around long threads stretched on a frame. The smaller the patterns, the harder it is for the fingers of men and women to tie knots of the right colours in the right places. So carpet-makers prefer the small and nimble fingers of children. It is now against the law for them to employ children of primary-school age, but many of them still do, both in factories and in the private homes where many of the best carpets are made.

Some of these private homes are the black woollen tents of nomad tribespeople who live in the high valleys during the summer, and on the warm coastal plains during the colder months. Hand-made carpets are the usual flooring for nomad tents, and they are often of a better quality and appearance

Part of the Tehran carpet market

than many machine-made Persian carpets sold at very high prices in other countries.

These nomads keep mainly to the fringes of the country, and have never been very popular with Iranian governments. They are fiercely independent, and so impatient of government interference that they are very hard to control. In the past, they often took the lead in rebellions. Even in recent times some of them have been bandits as well as herdsmen. Because of those things, and also because their hungry animals turn fertile land in semi-desert, the government has been trying to make them settle down as ordinary farmers. This campaign began long before the White Revolution, but was not very successful. However, the last Shah's father brought most of them under government control and stopped banditry—sometimes in very harsh ways. Since then the White Revolution has persuaded many of them that there might be some advantages in living a settled life.

The White Revolution was not the only revolution to change Iran sincle the 1950s. There has also been an industrial revolution—a change in the kind of work which earns the country most of its money, and a change in the ways that the work is done. Before 1960, nearly three-quarters of the money in Iran came from its crops and other farm products. By 1978 only about one third of the country's money was coming from farm work—and yet the farms were producing more than ever, for more money than ever.

If that seems hard to understand, the explanation is that there is now much more to the working life of Iran than crops, carpets and craft products. Iran is a rising industrial country, which relies on its factories rather than its farms and handicrafts to make it prosperous. So we may meet some surprises as we travel through the uplands, mountains and lowlands of modern Iran.

Uplands and Mountains

Running right across the north of Iran, mainly through the foothills of the Elburz Mountains, there is a modern road 2,000 kilometres (1,243 miles) long. This is Iran's section of Route A1 in the Asian Highway system, planned by the United Nations Organisation as a direct route through the whole continent of Asia, between Malaya in the far east and Turkey in the far west. In Turkey, it joins the European Highway, and so makes possible a comfortable car journey all the way across two continents, from the northern shore of Scotland to the southern shore of Singapore.

A highway bridge over a gorge in the Elburz Mountains

A general view of Tehran with the university in the foreground

Iran's part of Route A1 links the country with Turkey and Afghanistan. It passes through four of the most important Iranian cities, including the capital, Tehran. The other three —Tabriz, Qasvin and Mashad—are all very old cities. Each had its turn as capital while Tehran was hardly more than a village. But Tehran has now far outgrown them in size and in importance. With a rising population that should soon reach five million, it is much the biggest city in Iran, and the only city that has more than one million people. Tehran is also a very modern and international-looking city. Parts of it could almost be in western Europe if it were not for the signs in Arabic lettering, and the tall thin towers, called minarets, that rise over the bigger mosques. However, one of the city's newest buildings goes back to Iran's own ancient past for its style: the Shayyad Monument, a huge yet graceful archway, was built in 1971, to celebrate the 2,500th year since Cyrus the Great founded the old Persian empire.

Tehran people are also proud to show visitors their railway station, built in 1937. Iran had no railways until the 1930s, and seems to have given itself some magnificent stations to make up for the late start. Like the main railway line itself— from the Caspian Sea right to the Gulf—they were paid for wholly by a tax on tea and sugar. At that time, the oil-wells were not bringing in as much money as they do now, and Shah Reza would not allow his government to borrow from foreign countries. So perhaps it was just as well for people who needed the railway that Iranians are great tea-drinkers.

In a village to the south of Tehran, there is an old building which attracts foreign visitors not so much for its style or its beauty as for its name. It is called the Tower of Ala ad-Din, and you should not have to look very hard to see that the name has a link with a famous story. The link is a real one. The original story of Aladdin and his wonderful lamp comes from the set of old Iranian tales misleadingly called *The Arabian Nights Entertainments*.

Tehran did not need the magic of Aladdin's lamp to

become the centre of Iran's industrial revolution. Industries came to it naturally, because it was already the biggest city, the centre of government and transport, and within easy reach of useful raw materials—cotton from the farms, timber from the forests of the Elburz Mountains, and minerals such as copper, coal and iron from deposits spread widely over the uplands.

Before very long, the city was attracting too many industries. With factories overflowing into the small towns near by, it had become the largest industrial area in western Asia, while other Iranian cities could not provide work for all their people. So it was decided that the Tehran area should have no more factories. Anyone who wants to start a factory in Iran now must go to one of the other cities, or to a town at least 120 kilometres (75 miles) from Tehran.

This has meant that the other three cities on Route A1 have

Typical Iranian Muslim decoration in a mosque

also become centres of industry. At Tabriz—another city with a railway station that could be mistaken for one of the Shah's palaces—huge red-brick factories are making machine tools, diesel engines and tractors for use on the rich farmlands of the region where Noah planted his vineyard. At Qasvin, a city which the Prophet Mohammed is said to have called "a gate of the gates of Paradise", the main factories of a very large industrial estate turn out much of Iran's cement, and most of its glass. At Mashad, where every year about four million pilgrims come to pray under the golden dome of the country's holiest Muslim shrine, it seems at first that providing for the pilgrims and some tourists is the only industry. But among the glassy modern hotels and Iranian-style "bed and breakfasts" there are factories, too. Most of them deal with farm products from the surrounding province of Khorasan—grain, sugar-beet, cotton, leather and fruits.

Mashad also has an ancient craft industry that is very popular with pilgrims and tourists—cutting and setting gems from the turquoise that is mined in the province. In earlier times, visitors not only used to buy turquoise as jewellery for themselves and as presents, they also decorated the harness of their camels and horses with it. Turquoise was supposed to give protection on a journey by keeping off evil spirits.

The main turquoise mines are near the town of Neishabur, where the poet Omar Khayyam lived about nine hundred years ago. In Omar's time, Neishabur was much more

Decoration on the dome of the mosque at Mashad

important than it is now, but hardly anything is left of the
town that he knew. It was destroyed by one of the earthquakes
that are fairly common in this part of Iran.

Neishabur was also the home town of Faridoddin Attar,
who was a famous chemist of the Middle Ages. *Attar* is the
Iranian word for the oils which are distilled from flowers to
make perfumes; some people say that Faridoddin was given
the name because he invented a way of distilling the oil from
roses. That may not be true, but the perfume called attar of
roses was certainly invented many centuries ago in Iran,
which was then very well-known for its rose-gardens. The
official palace of the shahs in Tehran, now partly a museum,
has as its name the Iranian word for rose-garden—Golestan.

71

The spread of industry to the cities on Route A1 does not mean that the road has become a long ribbon of industrial development. In one section—between Tabriz and the Turkish border—there are only two small towns on 280 kilometres (170 miles) of highway. In another, where the road has passed below Tehran's most popular ski slopes and the snowy peak of Mount Damavand, it comes to the rice terraces and green fields of the Caspian Sea coast, and then climbs again to a famous and beautiful wildlife park. There, it follows a rushing river through a vast forested area where wild animals, birds and flowers are protected and cared for.

Outside the industrial zones, the rest of Route A1 runs through nearly 1,600 kilometres (1,000 miles) of open farmland, wooded valleys and steep rocky gorges, often with enormous bare mountains crowding in closely. The towns are far apart. Most of the mud-brick farming villages are well off the road. And the roadsides are left mainly to eating-houses and domed Muslim shrines—also far apart—and one or two old caravanserais.

Caravanserais were the "motels" of old Iran—and not so very far back in time. Less than a hundred years ago, the country had no long-distance roads that could be used by wheeled vehicles. Goods of all kinds—even pianos—were carried on the backs of camels and pack-horses. In groups of a hundred or more, they plodded one behind the other at the rate of about 32 kilometres (20 miles) a day. And at regular intervals along the main trade-roads they would come to a

Traditional village architecture in the uplands

caravanserai—a travellers' resting-place of rooms and stables built on all four sides of a square, gated courtyard.

Unlike the motels of today, most of the caravanserais were not run for profit. Shahs or local rulers had them built and looked after as a service to the travelling public. The government of modern Iran offers no such service to travellers, but it does provide picnic areas in pleasant roadside places, including the wildlife park. These, and most other handy places where it is possible to park a car and spread a carpet near water, are much used by Iranians from the town and cities—especially on Fridays.

Instead of the Jewish Saturday and the Christian Sunday, Muslims have Friday as their day of rest. If they take their religion seriously—as Iranians are now expected to do—they attend midday prayers in the mosques before they go picnicking.

But, wherever they are, and whatever they are doing, they must pause to pray at four other times during the day—not only on Fridays, but on every day of the week. When they are near a mosque, a voice from the minaret or the roof—sometimes through a loudspeaker—reminds them that it is prayer-time by crying: "There is no god but God, and Muhammad is his prophet".

For some people, afternoon picnicking is possible on any day of the week during summer, as their summer working-day starts around seven o'clock in the morning and ends at lunch-time. And in the warmer parts of the country the picnic season can begin as early as the New Year's Day holiday, called *Now Ruz*. That is because the new year in Iran starts on the first day of spring, which by the European calendar is 21st March in the northern hemisphere. The years are numbered differently, too. Iran follows the Muslim system of numbering from the year in which the Muslim Religion began, which means that the Christian year 1985 is the Muslim year 1363. Some Iranians also count years by the calendar of the old Persian Empire. So Iranians who go for road-side picnics in the year 1985 by European reckoning will do so in the old Persian year 2544.

Their picnics need not be on Route A1 of the Asian Highway. Modern motor roads that run roughly north and south now links the cities on Route A1 with other upland cities, and with the coastal Gulf area. Like the cities on Route A1, most of these other cities have become industrial centres since the 1950s.

They make motor vehicles, factory and farm machinery, cloth and clothing, chemicals, aluminium, electrical equipment, cement and other building materials—and very nearly all the other manufactured goods that a modern country needs.

Before the Second World War—and even in the first years after it—Iran had to import most of those things. Now, it is exporting some of them to other Asian countries, and to some countries in Africa and Europe. It also exports lead and zinc from its own mines. Where industries need metals as raw materials, most of those come from Iran's own mines, and are treated in one or other of its new industrial centres. For instance, Iranian iron ore and Iranian coal—as well as water from a new dam on the River Zayandeh—are being used to make steel in a huge new mill at Isfahan, the beautiful old capital city of Shah Abbas I. The mill was built and paid for by the U.S.S.R., in return for a supply of natural gas from the

An arched bridge across the river at Isfahan

wells near the Gulf. The gas travels to the Soviet Union through a pipeline 1,200 kilometres (745 miles) long, which also feeds gas to the upland cities.

However, although visitors will no doubt admire the Isfahan steel mill, they will probably be more interested in Isfahan melons. Excellent melons are grown in many parts of Iran, but those of the Isfahan area are so much tastier than the others that thousands from every harvest used to be packed in straw and sent by camel caravan to Tehran, more than 420 kilometres (260 miles) to the north.

Of course the visitor will also be interested in the magnificent buildings left by Shah Abbas I—mosques and minarets and

A covered street in the bazaar of Isfahan

palaces tiled in blue and green and gold, arched bridges over the river, and the great city square. A public square is the central feature of all old towns and cities in Iran, but the Maidan-e Shah (King's Square) in Isfahan has become famous both for its great beauty and its great size. It is the biggest city square in Asia, and very nearly the biggest in the world. In the time of Shah Abbas I, polo matches used to be played in it regularly. The stone goal-posts are still standing.

Behind an enormous gateway off the Maidan-e Shah spreads another of the city's famous features. This is the bazaar—a noisy crowded shopping area of narrow streets roofed over against the weather, and dimly-lit through openings in the roofs. Again, a bazaar is a feature of all old Iranian towns and cities, but here too Isfahan has the biggest. A visitor may easily lose himself as he wanders among shoppers not only buying all they need, but also watching much of it being made—spicy foods, sandals, cotton cloth hand-printed with designs carved on wooden blocks, jewellery, copper pots and kettles, tiny painted pictures (known all over the world as Persian miniatures), silver, gold and brass ware, the embroidered sheepskin jackets called pushtins, enamelled tiles and—of course—carpets.

The shoppers may also buy fruit. In upland Iran, fruits of many kinds are grown wherever there is water, but the province of Isfahan is the country's main fruit-growing area. Besides the famous melons, peaches, figs, apricots, nectarines, grapes and cherries are piled high in the bazaar. So too are dried fruits and nuts, both of which are now on Iran's growing list of exports.

When the fruit-trees are blooming in the spring, the fields of Isfahan province are also full of poppies. From these flowers come opium and other drugs which can help to cure illnesses when doctors use them in medicines, but are otherwise very dangerous. Because of these dangers, the government of Iran now keeps very careful control of poppy-growing and drug-making.

Far to the east of Isfahan, beyond the silk-making city of Yazd, there are two vast areas where it is impossible to grow anything at all except in a few oases. These are the upland deserts—wastes of sand and salt that have several names, but are usually called the Dasht-e Kavir and the Dasht-e Lut. In the Iranian language, *kavir* means salt, but in fact the Dasht-e Lut is the saltier of the two. Much of it has a thick surface of salt dried hard over deep mud, and is therefore very dangerous for anyone who tries to cross it. The salt can easily crack apart, like thin ice over water. Nothing lives in the Dasht-e Lut, not even a crawling insect, or a tiny weed. The Iranians have a legend that this desert, and not the Dead Sea area in Israel, is the place where Lot's wife was turned into a pillar of salt in the Bible story. That is why it is called the Dasht-e Lut, which means Desert of Lot.

Southward from Isfahan lies the wheat-growing province of Fars, the home of the Parsa tribe of Aryans who gave modern Iran its language, and from whom came the men who made the

Relief of the legendary Parsa king Jamshid who is believed to have ruled at Persepolis about five hundred years before Darius rebuilt the city

ancient Persian Empire. The university city of Shiraz—with some old buildings that nearly match those of Isfahan—is now the provincial capital. But 48 kilometres (30 miles) to the north lie the ruins of a city that was once more magnificent than either Shiraz or Isfahan. The city is Persepolis, reconstructed in around 500 B.C. by the empire-builder Darius the Great, as a fitting capital for the whole empire.

Darius was not content with building a city. Further north in the Zagros Ranges, he set a large army of workmen to flatten the face of a mountain, and then sent sculptors to carve on it not only an enormous figure of himself, but also the story of his reign in ancient cuneiform letters. People who know the cuneiform alphabet can still read every letter. Even those travellers who cannot read cuneiform can still pause to admire the majestic figure of Darius as they pass from the uplands to the lowlands.

Down to the Sea

When Darius had his image and his story carved on a Zagros mountain-face, the lowlands below the Zagros were wholly farming and grazing country. Nomads went to and from the mountains with the seasons, as they still do. Farmers tilled fields made fertile by irrigation from the rivers, as many are now doing again after long centuries of neglect. And if they sometimes saw dry ground suddenly burst into flames, they took it as a miracle worked by the gods, not as a sign of riches to come for Iran long after the empire had gone.

Even if they had known that the flames were a flare-up of natural gas pressing out from rock-layers far below them, and that where there is natural gas there is often oil too, it would have made no difference. It needed the inventions of the nineteenth century to make uses for the oil, and to reach it at the great depths where it lies sealed in porous rock. So it was not until 1908—2,400 years after Darius—that an Australian searcher struck oil in Khuzestan province, and gave the dry lands west of the Zagros an industry to compete with farming and grazing.

At first, Iran had a fairly small profit from its oil. Most of the money went to foreign companies which had been given the right to work the oilfields, But since 1951 an Iranian

The site of the first oil discovery in Iran

company, owned by the government, has taken over most of the fields. Although some foreign companies still work with the national company, the greater part of the profits now go to Iran.

Since Iran produces more oil than any country in the world except the U.S.A., the U.S.S.R. and Saudi Arabia, those profits are very large indeed. So the government has been able to pay for many new public services without taxing tea and sugar, as it did when the first railways were built. New schools and universities; better health services; improved roads; electricity supplies; radio, television and telephone networks; help for farmers; dams and piped water; air transport, and the stadium built in Tehran for the 1974 Asian Games have all come from the sale of oil. So too has the nationwide industrial development that is making Iran one of Asia's leading industrial countries.

Flames like these are the outward signs of oil and gas beneath the surface

In the oilfields area, there is more to industrial development than the oil-wells themselves. Some 64 kilometres (40 miles) from the mouth of the River Karun—as far as ships can go—stands the river port of Ahwaz. Ahwaz has now become a general industrial centre, with steel milling as its main industry.

Ahwaz is also the capital of Khuzestan province, but the "capital" of the oilfields is another river port, Abadan. Abadan, too, has a factory industry. It makes petro-chemicals —that is, chemicals which are extracted from oil (petroleum) for use in making fertilizers, plastics and detergents. But it is mainly the refining and exporting centre for crude oil which flows to it through pipelines from the oilfields.

However, the docks at Abadan are not big enough for the

enormous tankers which now carry oil round the world. Nor is the water deep enough, And it is the same with ports on the Gulf itself. Instead, an Iranian island in the Gulf—Kharg Island—has been turned into an oil-loading port at which the largest tankers afloat can berth. The oil comes to Kharg Island by undersea pipeline, and is loaded on to the tankers at the end of a concrete and steel "jetty" more than 1.5 kilometres (nearly one mile) long. Unfortunately for the oil industry, Kharg Island's terminal is at present unusable. It has been put out of action by Iraqi bombing. So, too, have the oil refineries at Abadan and Bandar Khomeini (formerly Bandar Shahpur).

Outside the Gulf, on the Gulf of Oman and fairly close to Iran's border with Pakistan, there is another new seaport, Chah Bahar. Chah Bahar is in the most remote corner of Iran, about 1,600 kilometres (1,000 miles) from Tehran, and is inhabited mainly by horse-riding tribesmen called Baluchi, who live in woven willow huts instead of tents. Inland, there are arid volcanic mountains, but some of the valleys and the coastlands are fertile, with a moist, tropical climate. Such tropical fruits as pineapples and bananas grow well here.

Chah Bahar is mainly a military base, but a training school for the Iranian merchant navy has recently started there, and the area is beginning to attract visitors who like remote places and warm sea-water. It could also develop a fishing industry, since fish of many kinds are plentiful, as they are in the Gulf waters. Fishing is an ancient industry in the Gulf, but it has grown much bigger with the opening of canning factories. Every year the factories turn out over ten million cans of fish, mainly tuna. But the Gulf is only a part of Iran's fisheries; there is also a large fishing industry off its northern coastlands, in the waters of the Caspian Sea.

The Caspian Sea is really an enormous lake, nearly as big as Spain, and half as big again as all the Great Lakes of North America. Its waters are salt, and in them live large numbers of the world's most valuable fish, the sturgeon. The sturgeon is a very big fish. It grows up to about three metres (ten feet) long, and can weigh as much as 450 kilograms (990 pounds). However, it is not the flesh of the sturgeon that makes it such a valuable fish. It is the masses of tiny blackish eggs found in most of the females. These eggs are cleaned and salted to make a food called caviare, which some people regard as a great

The waterfront at Abadan

Scene in a caviare-canning factory on the shore of the Caspian Sea

delicacy. Because the eggs from even the biggest sturgeon become only a small amount of caviare, very high prices are asked for it. Very rarely, the eggs are not blackish in colour, but golden.

The Caspian coastlands are very different from the rest of Iran, and not only because they are so much more wet, green and wooded. The village houses look different, too, and are rather more European in style than the mud-brick houses with flat or domed roofs on the other side of the Elburz Mountains. They are mainly two-storied, with sloping tiled roofs, walls of wood or stone, and sometimes a long balcony on the top storey. There are also houses that stand above the ground, on tall wooden piles.

Although most of these houses look more European than village houses in the uplands and the Gulf area, many of the people who live in them look slightly Chinese. They have

Fishermen with sturgeon caught in the Caspian Sea

inherited that appearance from the central Asian tribesmen who often invaded the area, and sometimes settled in it. Indeed, to the east of the Caspian Sea there is a whole community descended from central Asians. Called Turcomans, they speak their own language, and have only recently changed from nomadism (and sometimes banditry) to a settled life. In the same area is the Gorgan Plain, which was one of the first places where the last Shah sold his land to the farmers who worked it. Since then, a change to modern mechanized and scientific farming has resulted in wheat harvests three times bigger than they were before.

These lands to the east of the Caspian sea can be dry at

times—so dry that the scientific farmers of the Gorgan Plain often use artificial rain on their wheatfields. But no artificial rain is needed for the tea and rice of which Iranians are so fond. These grow on the terraced foothills above the Caspian's southern shore, and the moist, warm coastal plain that is partly below sea-level. Farmers here also grow oranges and other citrus fruits, and some raise silk-worms for the thread that is woven into silk cloth and stockings, mainly in the city of Rasht. Like Tehran and Isfahan in the uplands, Rasht also weaves a very large amount of cotton cloth. Throughout Iran, plain and printed cotton cloth is the main material for both men's and women's clothing.

There are also some newer industries in the Caspian area—mainly electrical—but the industrial revolution has been slow to reach this side of the Elburz Mountains. However, about 33,000 square kilometres (12,700 square miles) of the mountainsides are covered with a very valuable raw material—trees. These, and the country's other forests, are now national property. The government forestry department believes that they can be developed to make a timber industry that will be second only to oil production.

Meanwhile, it is oil that gives Iran its place in the modern world.

Iran in the World

Because no modern nation can do without oil and oil products, countries which can provide them have become very powerful. By threatening to withhold supplies, or to increase their prices greatly, these countries can influence the governments and industrialists of countries which have no oilfields, and perhaps force them into policies and actions which neither they nor the people like.

Under the Shah, Iran did not try to use its oil in this way. Nor was it greedy for extra profits. At meetings of the Organisation of Petroleum Exporting Countries (usually known as OPEC), it stood against the attempts of some members to force prices so high that they could cause business difficulties and unemployment in customer countries. However, it also stood against the lower prices which some other members would have liked to charge—and which all the buying countries wanted. This was because Iran depended on profits from oil sales to pay for the improvements that have come with the White Revolution.

As an Islamic republic, Iran is no less dependent on oil profits than it was under the Shah. Indeed, it is more dependent on them. It has to pay for a war which has already lasted four years and could last much longer, especially as the Iraqis are receiving help from the U.S.S.R. It has to pay for a planned programme of farming developments even more ambitious than Shah Mohammed Reza's White Revolution. It has to finance and manage all of its large industries, as these have been nationalised by the republican government. And, as a member of the Colombo Plan, it is committed to helping poorer Asian countries to develop their resources and improve their standard of living.

Added to all that, Iran's oil profits dropped very heavily after the oil industry was nationalised. This was partly because of war losses, and partly because the government took over the management of the industry at once, but did not have enough experience, technical knowledge or familiarity with the world's oil markets to keep the industry running as efficiently and profitably as the international oil companies had done.

However, production and profit figures have recently been climbing up again, and although these are still below the

Kharg Island, before it was bombed. The oil-loading jetty is in the foreground

In the aluminium works at Arak

pre-1980 level it seems certain that they will rise above it fairly soon, even though three oil refineries have been put out of action by Iraqi bombing. Iran has four other refineries, all in full production.

So far, and in spite of the war with Iraq, Iran's republican government seems to be following much the same independent policy on oil prices as the Shah's government did. It also appears to be following the Shah's policy of trying to keep a neutral and independent position in relation to the three powerful groups of countries which now seem to dominate international affairs.

These groups are the countries of the "Arab World", which include Iran's western neighbour and present enemy Iraq; the "Iron Curtain" countries, which include Iran's very powerful northern neighbour and old enemy the U.S.S.R., and the "Western Bloc" of European and American countries, with Israel and their other supporters.

Again Iran is very much opposed to any country which tries to interfere with the independence of another, and has made this clear in the United Nations Organisation, of which it was a founder member. Having had a very long struggle to keep their own independence, the Iranians are strongly sympathetic to those who have similar problems. Nor are they yet quite sure

A street in Isfahan. In the foreground is a mullah, typical of those who have been the country's leaders and rulers since it became an Islamic republic

that they are free of such problems themselves. Remembering their oil and the world's need of it, they must face the possibility that two, or even three, of these groups of nations could sink their differences and try to take control. When that happened during the First World War, an Iranian poet wrote: *Mush o gurba ke baham sakhtand dokkane attar kharab ast''* which means "The cat and the mouse have made friends, so the grocer's shop is ruined". Iran's main task in the world of today is to protect "the grocer's shop".

**An old photograph
of the last Shah
and his family**

Index